Case Handling
An Illustrated View from the Bench

H H Nicholas Chambers QC

Wildy, Simmonds & Hill Publishing

© Nicholas Chambers 2014

ISBN 9780854901470

British Library Cataloguing in Publication Data

A catalogue record for this book is available from the British Library

Chambers, N

Case Handling: An Illustrated View from the Bench

First published in 2014 by

Wildy, Simmonds & Hill Publishing
58 Carey Street
London WC2A 2JF
England

www.wildy.com

Contents

Acknowledgements   4

Foreword   5

Why am I Reading This?   6

Identifying the Problem   8

Is there a Case?   10

Strategy   12

Funding   14

Telling the Other Side   16

Responding   18

Correspondence   20

Litigants in Person   22

Settlement   24

Costs   26

Statements of Case   28

Directions and Case Management Conferences   30

Preliminary and Other Issues   32

Applications   34

Orders and Breaches of Orders   36

Problems   38

Disclosure   40

Witnesses   42

Expert Witnesses   44

Bundling   46

Skeletons and Authorities   48

Some Facts about Judges   50

Some Things that Judges Don't Like   52

Some Things that Judges Do Like   54

Acknowledgements

All thanks to Lord Thomas of Cwmgiedd for his generous foreword and thanks to his Personal Assistant Michèle Souris for her kind help. Andy Allanson of Tresco Studios did his magic with the computer and Derek Brown of Oblong Creative Ltd was wonderfully deft in design. Giles Caldin brought style and wit. HHJ Charles Harris QC provided a depth of dry wisdom and Kyle Lawson of Brick Court Chambers a thoughtfully youthful perspective. Duncan Aldred of CMS Cameron McKenna annotated my offerings with cursive authority. Vicky Pittman and Sarah Randall of OUP have been truly patient. Gavin Wells of Ede & Ravenscroft showed me all sort of robes that are more complicated than they appear. The United States Postal Service gave inspiration. Brian Hill of Wildy, Simmonds & Hill has been as generous as ever with his time, knowledge and help. My family brought a kindly indulgence and useful eye for detail. I remember with affection all the members of the Bench and Court Service with whom it was such a pleasure to work.

The author's profits go to the Barristers' Benevolent Association.

Foreword

In *Missed Moments in Legal History* Nick Chambers provided us with a delightful collection of watercolours, illustrating historical events and significant cases in the development of the law. They were, as Lord Neuberger described them, "a collection of clever counterfactual vignettes". The last watercolour was captioned, "A court takes part in a Ministry of Justice pilot project to reduce the cost of civil litigation". As the observations as to what really happened point out, we have tried almost everything else other than the Ouija board illustrated in the watercolour.

That watercolour has led on to the current collection where Nick Chambers has brought to bear his years of experience as a distinguished practitioner and highly respected judge in providing excellent advice on every stage of litigation. From his time as the Mercantile Judge for Wales and Chester, he no doubt learnt an old Welsh saying, "*Ysgol Bryd Ysgol Brofiad*" which roughly translated means "the school of experience is an expensive one". He adapts this slightly in his explanation as to "Why am I reading this?" by saying, "Because it is better to learn from a book (with pictures) than bitter experience".

Those wise enough to acquire and read this book will find an invaluable, incisive and fun guide as to the conduct of litigation. Some is very broadly based, such as the advice on strategy and funding, but other sections give advice which it would be foolish to ignore. For example the guidance on correspondence between parties to litigation gets over the message that each letter should be written with a view to it being read in court at the end of a long day in a hot July. What might seem clever and amusing at the time it was written certainly appears in a very different light when read out at such a time.

In his advice on skeletons and authorities, I very much hope that he succeeds where so many others have failed. The seventh paragraph is particularly worthy of attention.

He winds the advice off with a section on judges – some facts about judges, some things that judges do like and some things judges don't like. It is always important to remember, "For most – probably all – judges a pinch of merit is worth a peck of law!".

Much has been written setting out advice to the young advocate or litigator. This short and delightfully illustrated book contains a collection of wisdom which few, however experienced they may be, would not greatly benefit from reading.

The Right Hon. The Lord Thomas of Cwmgiedd
Lord Chief Justice of England and Wales

Why Am I Reading This?

Because judges see cases that were wrong from the start.

Because judges see cases that went wrong after the start.

Because judges don't always know what went wrong.

Because judges need help in not getting things wrong.

Because you need to be ready to conduct trials in court and advise from the start.

Because this book is about the basics so you don't have to read lots of footnotes.

Because it is better to learn from a book (with pictures) than bitter experience.

Because you are in charge.

Why am I reading this?

Identifying the Problem

Every case involves a problem – find out what it really is.

What is the issue?

The client may feel angry, betrayed, got at, giddily aloft on the moral high ground, shiftily aware of the moral low ground, utterly confident of the rightness of his, her or its position without quite knowing what that position is.

Remember that the client is not always a reliable witness.

Listen

Clarify

Find out what the client wants.

Establish what the client needs.

Sometimes the most important information comes almost as an afterthought – "I don't suppose this is important but . . .".

Identifying the problem

Is there a Case?

Every case involves a problem but not every problem involves a case.

What does the client want?

Okay, something went wrong but what is the potential relief – damages, an injunction, restitution, a declaration ...?

What are the chances of getting it?

Do you know the relevant law?

Have you got some reliable evidence?

Is there a defence better than blind faith? If so, what is it?

Be objective – most cases have a pattern. Trying to mix and match a case into existence by picking a bit of evidence here and a bit of evidence there is not a good idea.

Is there a case?

Strategy

Remember that all that follows must be done with the client's involvement and consent.

Where do you want to go?

How are you going to get there?

What team are you going to use?

What, if any, use is going to be made of counsel – an embedded part of the team or there as and when required?

The chances are that your dispute will settle, so how are you going to get the best terms?

What are the difficulties?

How will you address them?

Are you up to date with the law?

Are you up to date with procedure?

How are you going to manage the documents? Do you need a document management system?

Who will be on your internal contact list?

What are your plans B, C, D, E, F ...?

Mediation?

Arbitration or Court?

Plan long, be proactive if possible and effectively reactive if necessary.

The better your strategy the better your control.

Plan, plan, plan – and do it.

But always remember that once the battle begins the strategy usually ends; so be flexible.

Strategy

Funding

Where is the money coming from?

Funders want to be told clearly what the case is about.

Funders don't like fancy cases with lots of unsettled law and principle.

Funders want to know what a case is worth. Do you know what your case is worth?

Funders want to know when they are going to get their cut. Do you know when that will be?

Funders want settlements not the Supreme Court.

Funders don't like surprises.

Funding

Telling the Other Side

Who is your intended reader?

Abusive letters dripping with moral fervour do not impress.

Set out your case clearly, courteously and firmly.

Say what you want and why you want it.

Don't resort to generalities.

Don't set out useless detail.

Be relevant.

If you are following a pre-action protocol say so and do what the protocol requires.

You are setting the tone for all that follows.

Telling the other side

Responding

Abusive letters dripping with moral fervour do not impress nor does sarcastic dismissiveness.

Identify the problem and address it firmly and courteously.

If you are following a pre-action protocol do what the protocol requires in the time that is stated.

It might help to send a sensible without prejudice letter along with your open letter.

You are setting the tone for all that follows.

Responding

Correspondence

The purpose of correspondence in litigation is to communicate in a sensible and constructive way. It can be of great use later – especially in respect of costs.

Solicitors' correspondence is not a judge's favourite bedtime reading but can be very revealing of conflicts with the case presented at trial.

Be relevant and courteous – you never know when you might want a favour in return.

Respond promptly and sensibly to offers to mediate – win or lose a failure to do this could be very expensive.

Without prejudice correspondence should be clearly marked "without prejudice".

Do you really know what "without prejudice" means?

Open correspondence should not refer (even inferentially) to without prejudice exchanges.

Correspondence includes your own side – keep the client fully informed and you instructions up to date.

Confirm conversations in writing.

Copy emails to the current personal assistant, paralegal or trainee – the main addressee may be unavailable.

Be careful with your spelling and grammar – bad spelling and grammar are sources of needless irritation.

A casually slavish use of spell check can get results almost as surprising as Sat Nav.

Think before you press the send button.

Correspondence

Litigants in Person

If you are not a litigant in person:

Many litigants in person become involved in litigation because they have no alternative and many others become involved in litigation because they think that they have no alternative.

While you are perfectly entitled to be as firm as the circumstances require you should be unfailingly courteous.

Try to find what the real issues are and address them.

It is your duty to all litigants in person to do what you can to assist them with the mechanics of the process of litigation such as (to the extent that you are permitted) helping with the orderly compilation of hearing bundles.

Expect to feel that it is frustratingly as if the court is bending over backwards in favour of your opponent.

If you are a litigant in person:

Try to identify the real issues.

Address the issues in ordinary English – there is no such language as "Courtspeak".

Don't download statements of case from the internet without understanding what they say and being able to support what is said at a hearing – the judge will be looking at you not the website.

Remember that asserting something is not the same thing as proving it.

Always obey court orders and, if you may be late, immediately apply for an extension of time or an adjournment with your reasons and (where needed) the evidence for doing so.

Take a good note.

Litigants in person

Settlement

The chances are that you will settle so what are you going to do about it?

Early settlement should mean cheaper settlement.

Settlement brings certainty. You can never be sure how a trial will go.

The longer you wait to settle the greater the tension between dealing with the costs and dealing with the claim.

Orderly settlement gives an orderly outcome – what will be the best way of going about it? Between counsel; between solicitors; between clients?

Mediation is one of a number of ways of achieving your goal. You could start by picking up the telephone – wp of course.

Have you read "The Jackson ADR Handbook"? If not, why not? If yes, how are you going to use it?

Be proactive – use offers.

Inquiring about settlement is not a sign of weakness – pleading for settlement is.

It is your job to explain to the client that cases fought as a matter of principle have a way of ending in disaster – how you do it is up to you.

Have you a shopping list of what you need to deal with? What are you settling? Who is getting what? What is going to happen to costs? What about interest? ...

Remember that under most mediation agreements there is only a settlement if there is a signed agreement.

Who is the decision maker for each party?

Keep your client informed and manage expectations.

Settlement

Costs

Litigation should not be about costs but much too often it ends up that way.

Protect your position with suitable offers – Part 36 and otherwise – right from the start or even before it.

Review your offers as you go along.

Remember the terrible things that can happen if you don't get your costs budget in on time.

Remember the terrible things that can happen if you do get your budget in on time but it is a useless budget.

Remember you will never get all your costs back.

Remember judges can be a little random with costs because most Circuit and High Court Judges know next to nothing about them.

Remember that getting involved in a detailed costs assessment is like entering the Sixth Circle of Hell.

Remember to keep your client fully informed on costs – all aspects of litigation (including communicating with the client) can cost much more than the client expects with uncomfortable consequences unless prepared for.

Remember that costs orders can be as difficult to enforce as judgments.

Costs

Statements of Case

A statement of case is a statement of case – a succinct statement of what is necessary to establish the case.

If you are the claimant start (in your mind) at the end – what are you asking for?

Once you know what you are asking for, write down what you need in order to get it.

What is the story?

What is the law?

If you are a defendant – what is your defence?

You can only not admit an allegation if you really don't know if it is correct.

You can only deny an allegation if you are prepared to say why.

A reply is a reply to the defence not a chance to add something you forgot to put in the particulars of claim.

If you want to add something that you forgot to put in the particulars of claim make an amendment or, if appropriate, serve voluntary further information.

If you need to amend do it as soon as you can and give good warning as soon as you can.

Give the particulars you need to give – if you are alleging a conversation say when, where and between whom it took place with the gist of the words used – if you are relying on documents identify them.

Do not allege dishonesty without giving particulars in support of the allegation.

Don't have pages of sub-paragraphs with no clear indication of the paragraph to which they belong.

Statements of case

Directions and Case Management Conferences

What is the case about?

What are you going to need? How many witnesses of fact? What experts? How heavy is the documentation likely to be?

Do you want a schedule or two?

Of course you can give a reasonable estimate of how long the trial should last so give it – diaries need dates.

Err on the side of caution – witnesses can take longer than advocates think.

Don't fiddle around. You will need to mediate or have a good reason not to; so decide your position now. You should know if you need an expert and, if so, what sort; so get it in the directions.

Timetables should neither be absurdly optimistic nor too pessimistic.

Have you consulted the other side about completing the directions questionnaire?

Do you both want a short stay to see if you can sort out the dispute?

Can the order be done on paper?

If there is the least doubt then have a hearing but why not have a conference call?

Don't get too excited – you are not in the playground.

Who is going to draw the order?

Make sure there can be no doubt about what was ordered or agreed. Even the tape is not always clear.

Remember that you will need the approval of the court to an agreed order for directions.

Directions and case management conferences

Preliminary and Other Issues

Forget the dogma – the trouble with preliminary issues is that, when they go wrong, they go very wrong indeed.

When they go wrong they cost a mint of money – nobody quite knows what has been decided or why anyone should have wanted it decided in the first place.

From first to last a preliminary issue must be completely clear – you can change it as you go along but only if everyone knows where they are.

The function of a preliminary issue is to save time and money by clarification. Is there a contract? What does the contract mean? Is there liability?

Do not base a preliminary issue on assumed facts – someone will always say that the real facts are different and the finding has no application.

If you cannot be sure that the preliminary issue will do what it should do have a proper trial.

For the rest – a list of issues is fine as long as it does not become a pleading.

A list of issues is there to provide a useful framework not hoops of steel.

Preliminary and other issues

Applications

Don't make an application unless you have to. Start with sensible emails or letters. You might even pick up the phone.

Applications can be very expensive.

Applications have a way of developing lives of their own and can cause long delays.

Applications have special rules of proof that sometimes favour the applicant and sometimes the respondent. It might be better to go for an early trial date than try for summary judgment. It might be a good idea to offer an undertaking.

Be clear what you are asking for and why you should have it.

Be prepared with the necessary supporting evidence.

Be frank.

The price for the early hearing of an urgent application may be a judge who knows nothing about that area of the law – be ready to help.

Give a realistic estimate and be ready to do everything you need to do in the time that you are given.

Be clear why you are opposing an application and have such evidence as you can marshal to do so.

Witness statements are far more effective if they state the facts without the addition of qualitative language – nobody cares if you were "horrified" at the "appalling" behaviour of the other side and it only provides an invitation to the other side to descend to the same level.

Witness statements are not arguments. Their purpose is to set out the evidence that supports the argument – not always an easy distinction. Use headings that show that you know the requirements in question. If you are alleging non-disclosure say so and why so without listing the authorities.

It is the witness's statement not yours – don't make your client sound like a lawyer.

Applications

Orders and Breaches of Orders

Orders are there to be obeyed – they are not aspirational.

These days the consequences of not obeying an order can be truly dire.

So first of all do what you can to make sure that the order requires you to do what you can do within a time that you can fairly do it. Even the most condign of orders in the most serious of situations can be tweaked a bit if you address the court with charm and the appearance of reason.

Never wait until it is too late.

Most orders can be complied with, the usual problem is the time needed. It won't be all right on the night – if you need an extension always ask for it as soon as possible with your best reasons why.

Allow for practical problems. Documents always take longer to prepare than you think they will. Courts aren't impressed by the computer going down ten minutes before the deadline when there were three weeks in which to meet it.

Don't be too clever by half – if you have permission to serve a reply out of time that is not permission to serve new particulars of claim.

Try to avoid unless orders. The need to establish whether there has in fact been a breach and the need to apply for relief from sanction will soak up time and expense.

Be careful of consent orders – they can be difficult to alter.

If you are in breach of an order immediately do all that is necessary to address the situation including doing what you were first ordered to do.

Orders and breaches of orders

Problems

Never keep a problem to yourself if it could be too big for you to deal with.

Find out before ever you have such a problem to whom you could go if it came your way. If there is nobody, go and work somewhere else.

Never think a problem will solve itself – sometimes they do but don't count on it.

Err on the side of caution – the situation could be even worse than you think or you might make it so.

Think things through. Why is it a problem? How might it be sorted out? The person you confide in will want to know and you will be seen as a sensible person trying to address a difficult matter in a sensible way.

Where courts are concerned, be frank and try for the best result consistent with your having done so.

Where the other side is concerned, don't attempt to defend the indefensible.

Many disasters occur for pretty obvious reasons.

Problems

Disclosure

You cannot start too early to think about disclosure.

Disclosure is not an invitation to start a cottage industry nor is it the legal profession's answer to shelf stacking.

Proper disclosure is an exercise in intelligence and commonsense.

The questions are simple. What are the issues? What is there and was there (for good or bad) that is relevant to the resolution of those issues?

Answering the questions is not so easy – particularly as it is your call.

So, if in doubt, get advice and if you can't get advice, err on the side of caution.

Don't throw in everything you can grab just because you can't be wrong if you throw everything in can you?

Well yes you can be because disclosure is very expensive and someone will have to pay and these days clients are a bit picky about that sort of thing.

If you are going to have electronic disclosure be sure to agree a protocol that won't have to be changed. Changes are expensive. Should you use an expert?

Remember to deal with what the client once had in its control.

Disclosure is a time for evaluating your case. What do your documents show? What don't they show? Even more so, what do or don't the other side's documents show?

Disclosure is a continuing obligation.

Disclosure

Witnesses

Don't accept "X will say, prove, support this that or the other" – go and find out.

Listen.

Use the witness's own words and own account – that is what will come out in cross-examination.

Take the witness to the documents even if he or she finds it tedious.

Address the issues – no one is interested in private agendas.

Don't waste time on what is not in dispute.

Don't annex documents to a witness statement – keep them separate.

Check availability clearly and in good time – mistakes can be expensive.

If you can't get a witness to court, check video links and Skype though remember that they don't appeal to every judge.

Is your witness (who may be your client) going to be any good? If not, what are you going to do about it?

Check if your witness has any special needs – if so, arrange for them to be addressed practically and discreetly.

Any allegation of dishonesty against a witness must be clearly made.

Any allegation of dishonesty against a witness should never be made without good grounds for doing so.

Coaching a witness is absolutely out but preparing a witness for the experience of being in court (and only that) is another matter.

Witnesses

Expert Witnesses

Do you need one, two, three, four ...? Why?

What is the expert's expertise? To what is that expertise going to be applied?

Is the issue susceptible to the uncontroversial application of necessary expertise? If so, why not use a joint expert?

If all you need is someone good with figures don't instruct an expert geared to provide something much more sophisticated at a price to match.

If the issue is controversial and you are worried about what a joint expert might say, ask to be allowed to instruct a separate one from the start.

What about sequential reports?

Make sure your instructions clearly address what the expert is being asked to do.

Can you understand the report? Can you understand the reasoning in the report? Do the conclusions answer the questions that you want answered?

How good is the other side's expert evidence?

Are the experts fulfilling their duty to assist the court?

Is it time to have a chat with the other side?

Where needed, keep your reports up to date.

Expert witnesses

Bundling

Bundling is expensive so prepare well.

Discuss the makeup of the bundle with all other parties – A4, A5, discs, online . . .?

If there is a governing bundling guide or practice direction follow it.

Don't cram a lever arch file like a piece of holiday luggage.

Do make sure that your lever arch files are as robust as any good piece of holiday luggage.

Slim amounts of paper should sit in slim lever arch files.

Never trust a clip file to hold any quantity of paper.

Judges with lever arch files that don't work are inclined to be irritable.

Like toothache a defective file won't improve until it is attended to.

Judges hate staples.

You can never mark a file in too many places – front, spine, inside cover ...

Put the bundle together in a nice clear order with a nice clear index. Do put dividers between different subject matter. Don't put dividers between every document in the chronological bundle. The earliest date comes first not last.

Try to make email threads as user friendly as possible.

Provide all other parties with a fully paginated bundle.

Don't supply slabs of updates for the judge to sort out.

If you do have to supply updates, hole punch them and make it clear where they go.

Bundling

Skeletons and Authorities

You have read what just about every judge in the Court of Appeal has to say about skeletons and authorities — so why on earth don't you do it?

It's because you're scared — scared that somewhere there is a point that you'll have left out — scared that there might be something in that authority even if you can't see what it is — scared because otherwise something might be said at the hearing which will lead those behind you to say or (just as bad if not worse) think that you were (a) idle and/or (b) stupid.

So what you do is treat the whole thing like an advanced exercise in disclosure — chuck everything in then you can't be wrong can you?

The trouble is you can.

Skeletons and authorities are the tools of persuasion.

Unlike disclosure the judge has to read every last word of your skeleton and have a fair idea of your authorities.

The skeleton is your chance to tell the judge what the case is about, what you want and why you should have it in no more than the time taken between the judicial supper and bed; much less if possible. If you get it wrong and the other side get it right they are already ahead.

As to authorities — these days many judges are terrific swots and most leading cases contain a short thesis on the relevant law. There are judges who know all about the construction of contracts and have no hesitation in telling us. There is no need to do all that work again. Even less is there a need to take the court through it all again. Make sure you have the latest relevant authorities (including the ones that don't help you) and you will usually have done all that is needed.

Skeletons and authorities

Some Facts about Judges

All judges are human.

Although they have many things in common all judges are different.

The judge's job is to deal with cases fairly and expeditiously.

Judges can see almost everything going on in court and also hear quite a lot of it.

Many judges like to pitch into the argument regardless of where you are in your submissions.

Many judges like asking witnesses lots of questions including some they really should not.

Some judges like law and some don't. Some judges know the law and some don't. Some judges admit that they don't know the law and some don't.

For most – probably all - judges a pinch of merit is worth a peck of law.

Clever judges don't always get it right. Even nice judges can do some rather strange things.

Some judges read all the papers and some don't. All judges read the skeleton arguments.

A judge's findings of fact are rarely overturned.

Judicial discretion correctly applied is beyond attack.

Most judges respond well to kindness and tact.

Trial judges are not counsellors or mediators – by the time a case gets that far someone is right and someone is wrong.

Judges will know if you behave badly to court staff.

Some facts about judges

Some Things that Judges Don't Like

Irrelevance especially prolix irrelevance

Obtuse answers to clear questions

Vulgar abuse wherever directed

Bundles which are not in chronological order and properly paginated and which break up correspondence.

Endless useless authorities

Out of date authorities

Useless questions especially when repeated.

Failure to put the relevant parts of the case to a witness.

Repeatedly putting a case to a witness when it has been clearly rejected.

Not being responsive to the witness's answers.

A cross-examination file showing a startlingly number of pages to come when most things seem to have been dealt with.

Blaming the witness for overrunning the time estimate.

Trickiness   Sulkiness   Sarcasm   Obstructiveness

Being copied in on everything

Lack of commonsense

Failure to heed warnings that time is running out.

Untangling email threads – though they often give the answer to the dispute.

Attempts to rewrite the findings set out in a draft judgment.

Being asked for the moon when you would be lucky to get anything.

Some things that judges don't like

Some Things that Judges Do Like

Good skeleton arguments with a well prepared bundle

Trustworthiness   Moderation   Commonsense   Humour

Being told what the hearing is really about

Helpfulness to the Bench and the other side

Concession when concession should be made

Incisive cross-examination

Clear arguments that are well made

Courtesy to witnesses

The pursuit of a relevant line of questioning with clarity and economy

Clearly putting relevant matters in cross-examination when following the principle that witnesses must be given a proper opportunity to deal with matters where their evidence is controversial or their integrity is being challenged.

Asking one question at a time

Intelligent reaction to a witness's answers

Clear arguments that are well made

Being referred to the relevant parts of relevant authorities

Graceful acceptance of adverse decisions

Prompt permissible corrections to draft judgements

Charm and tact with ushers

People who have hole punches, diaries and calculators and know the correct reference for the next document to be added to the bundle.

Some things that judges do like